Mind of a Mad Black Man

Mind of a Mad Black Man

The Thoughts, Views, & Random Banter of a Slightly Unbalanced Black Man

By

Jamal M. Jones

Foreword by Jacqueline B. Rampey

Edited by Norma Brown-Harris & Janice Harpaul-Jones

dotted eye
Multimedia & Publishing Group

Texas

Published by Dotted Eye Multimedia & Publishing Group, LLC, Texas.
No part of this book may be used or reproduced in any manner whatsoever without written, recorded, or otherwise documented permission except in the case of brief quotations embodied in critical articles, reviews, commentaries, or educational references.

This book may be purchased for educational, business, personal, or sales promotional use.

For all inquiries and information please contact: Marketing@Dotted-Eye.com
Or write:
Attn: Publishing Marketing Department
Dotted Eye Multimedia & Publishing Group, LLC
P.O. Box 5781
Round Rock, TX 78683-5781

Library of Congress Cataloging-in-Publication Data is available.

ISBN-13: 978-0-6151-8369-5

Cover design & Book design: Dotted Eye Multimedia & Publishing Group, LLC

www.Dotted-Eye.com
www.MindofAMadBlackMan.com

Printed in the United States of America

~ Dedication ~

This collection of poems is dedicated to life's experiences; my parents and their lessons, my sister and the inspiration that her growth has brought me; to my boys, who have taught me about manhood and the joys of fatherhood; my friends who have supported me through the thickest and thinnest of times. Mostly I dedicate this book to my wife, the woman who has given me reason to truly understand and enjoy love, but has also taken the time to truly understand me while we have worked to redefine the concept of love.

Contents

"You make plans and God laughs"

... Words from my Father

Moving Foreword

I met Jamal when he was 3 and I was 4; that's almost as long as I've known myself, and as long as I've know my real brothers. We all grew up "next-door-neighbors" the old fashioned way, borrowing cups of sugar and sharing the bar-b-q grill. I think it was ours. The Joneses moved in next door to us shortly after we moved to the tree-lined 228th street in Cambria Heights, Queens. My first memory of him is him running full speed from the back of the house to the front where my dad was introducing his dad to me as "Mr. Mike," because it was easier than "Mr. Miguel," and less formal than "Mr. Jones," and what's the use of so much formality between houses only 6 feet apart. Jamal had a huge fro, the way lots of 3 year old black boys do before their parents let go of the notion that keeping the baby's hair long will keep him a baby. Jamal has not cut his son's hair either, and his fro makes him look just like his dad 29 years ago. Maybe he is waiting for him to run out of the backyard at full speed on their new, tree-lined street in Austin; and maybe he will introduce him to the neighbor's kid who will call him "Mr. Jones" because their houses are further apart.

Knowing Jamal for so many years doesn't necessarily mean knowing him better, it just means knowing him longer. He changes. He grows. He gets more complex...mature, like "not-quite-finished-aging" wine. He reaches new frontiers and attacks new endeavors with focus and animalistic determination, with all the grace and beauty of a lion on a gazelle. This book is raw Jamal; it is his life; his reality and his fantasy, his history and his present, his heart and his mind, his hip and his hop. It is his love and his anger, his controversy and his comedy; you laugh and cry and dap him up and repeat him to your peoples. I teach him to my students. These poems and words get inside your mind and your mouth as he takes what you wanted to say, tried to say, and puts it together in the way that you could not; and romances your girl for you, or from you, as he schools you about life and love and words.

Come along for the ride into the galaxy that is Jamal; expansive in his outlook and scope, yet real and personal in language and connection. You know this guy; you went to high school with him, played ball, lit firecrackers in the alley, laughed and lied about your conquests and non-quests with him. His life is on these pages; naked and exposed. You see him but you also see yourself in these lines; you remember living this way, loving this way. Step into the *Mind of a Mad Black Man* and reconnect with yourself.

We have a running joke in my family that we are trying to keep up with the Joneses. We are. Jamal taught me in our early teen years that there is no such thing as luck- simply preparation meeting opportunity. The compilation of these works is evidence of that idea. This book is 32 years in the making; 31 ½ living, and 6 months from plan to publishing and preparation for the next one. This is just the beginning, the first dose to whet your appetite, but take it slow and enjoy because he has to live it to write it and tell it to you this way again.

Jacqueline B. Rampey

The Un-Epilogue: From Mouth to Ear

When I approached this part of the book, I found it to be more challenging than actually writing the poems. The status quo for this section is to generally speak about yourself and inspirations. I imagined myself sitting in an interview and being asked, "So, tell me a little bit about yourself." I recall sitting in the offices of interviewing managers thinking to myself, "Please don't ask me to tell you a little bit about myself." Other than my evident desire for a job, how can I summarize thirty plus years of life growing into a black man in a few sentences? You never know exactly what to say. It's your opportunity to put your best foot forward or sound just like any other person. You don't want to run down your entire resume or write an autobiography, but you do want to make yourself sound better than average.

I consider myself to be rather accomplished as a black male in today's version of the United States. Born in Brooklyn and raised in Queens, New York, I've completed high school, college, earned an MBA, never been arrested, have a good job, have started a business with a couple of friends, failed at a business with a couple of friends, have a three year old son, a sixteen year old step son, married to an amazing Jamaican-born woman whom I love immensely, and have a tight knit family that has helped me through the most challenging periods of my life. The corporate America thing isn't half bad. It pays the bills, keeps food in my family's stomach, a roof over our heads, and gives me something to do forty to fifty hours out of the week. Occasionally I actually find myself enjoying what I do.

As I look back, while driving back and forth between New Jersey and New York, I found the time to fall in love with my wife, who recently accompanied me on a journey to Austin, Texas. In addition to that, I managed to document the thoughts and emotions I have experienced over the last ten years of my life; a period that captures my transformation into manhood. *Mind of a Mad Black Man* represents the first portion of that journey...a struggle to exit my twenties while dealing with relationships, career, social challenges, and a growing evolution into the role of man...a black man. As I sit huddled in my cubicle, secretly typing this introduction camouflaged by work related content, I think about my second poetry manuscript, as well as the beginning of a biography that serves as a satirical and introspective review of my life as only I can recall it. How the hell did I get here?

I've always liked to write. I used to write an occasional "Roses are red, violets are blue, candy is sweet, but not sweeter than you" poem when I was younger. When I reached high school, most of my friends had begun to DJ. Every one of us had two broken turntables, a milk crate with the summer's hottest albums, a microphone, or two headphones; one plugged into the microphone jack and one plugged into the headphone jack. I on the other hand couldn't afford to keep up with all of the newest music singles that came out on a weekly basis, and opted to write rhymes instead. I occasionally wrote a rap that due to inconsistent lyrics could never actually flow with a beat. It then became a poem. I wrote throughout high school and college and was sometimes predicted by friends to be a next raw act. Around the time I was about to graduate from Morgan State University, I began to write rhymes less and started to write poetry more often. Less thug, more love. I assume that the whole vision of being the hip-hop industry's newest phenom faded away with maturity. And so began the love and joy of writing poetry.

Until I actually drafted my manuscript I had no idea that I had created enough pieces to reach this point. You know how you think about doing something, but don't realize how capable you are of doing it until you are half way there. Well, in this case, I didn't realize it until it was finished; years later after I sat down and opened the file folder filled with nothing but words from my youth and experience. Now in my thirties I look back at this and chuckle, finding humor in experiences I believed to be so challenging at the time. I find it calming to laugh at myself and everyone around me. I've always worn my emotions on my sleeves, but made sure they were protected with metal-spiked bracelets. Growing up in a nuclear home, among friends who referred to me as a "Cosby Kid," and having a family that wasn't openly dysfunctional, I had to wait until my own adulthood birthed mentionable challenges and stories that were worth writing about.

I realized that my sometimes distorted and boarder-line demented thought processes, were often reflected in my secret life as an aspiring rapper. My family and friends would read or hear my lyrics and wonder where the aggression came from. I would email friends lyrics that I had written with the hidden agenda of becoming the first rapper discovered via email. It didn't work out that way. Raps morphed into rhymes, rhymes were too deep to be raps, and as I matured, my flow matured into a fusion of the two which represented the likeness of a pen, a pad, drums from African chants, baselines from Jazz, violins from pain and sorrow, and squelching microphones crossed in front of loud speakers at Rap concerts. These elements, accompanied by random long-windedness, and a tendency to write exactly what was on my mind instead of speaking it, left me with nothing left to do except write. I wrote for anger. I wrote for joy. I wrote for love, hate, introspectiveness, and humor. I wrote for those who wouldn't. Mostly I wrote for myself. My poems serve as documentation of my story...an abridged version of my biography, in which the reader is only privy to the emotion and thought behind the experience.

Life is a collection of poems where I express my abstract understanding and awareness of social issues, experiences, and life's lessons. *Love* is a realistic description of feelings and love that I, along with friends, have encountered during our early years as independent adults. *The Words* are a compilation of my failed attempts at starting a few books. Sometimes you get an idea to write about something that you feel emotionally and socially attached to. But after a page or so, you realize that you've got about two hundred pages left to go. You look back at the first few paragraphs and notice that you have already summarized everything that had crossed your mind. The last few lines are usually spent trying to smoothly end what you've started.

Prelude to Sleeplessness represents the introduction to my next book. Not only does it provide insight into another phase of my life, but a new sense of alertness and an awakening to where I am now. Through all three of these chapters, I felt it fair to not only show you where I've been, but where I am, as well as where I'm going.

Hopefully you enjoy what you read. I'm not sure if this will be the last you've heard of me or not. However, if in fact it is, it was a pleasure to provide these few pages for your perusal. If I do have the luck of dropping another collection of words into your hands, I will see you again. Until then, grow from life, grow from love, and grow from the words that express them.

Have a seat. Start counting backwards from 10...

Part 1: Life (līf)

1: The interval of time between birth and death.[1]

2: The cereal Mikey used to eat. (But he'll eat anything)

Visualize

Visualize

As I walk through the valley

Looking up to the left and the right

Seeing the two sides of thought

The good and bad to every story

the light and dark of every day

The nigga and the bitch

the motha' and the fucka'

The pimp, the hoe

My alter ego

As I raise hell in this heaven

Imagination pollutes the purity of my youth

Puberty robs me of my innocence

in a world that forbids sin

And a man wearing a robe covering his black clothes

tells me to "repent"

for thoughts his God has allowed me to think

Telling me that my God is all knowing

all powerful

Then free my mind, free my soul

Take me to the motherland

The Promised Land

The pearl white gates

where people who follow the light usually go

Show me the way to serenity

Without leaving me at the door when we get there

I want to see what you've been telling me about

What you've been preaching and shouting

Bragging about this so-called "Creator"

But when I call his name

you tell me that I've used it in vein

To question his existence is sinful

But to have no conscience is pitiful

I am individual

So I visualize things that have been on my mind

I see Him as neither He nor She

but a part of me that is meant to be free

2.5 Million Served

Sitting in McDonalds

an old man sits at my table and begins to talk to me

While cleaning off the garbage on the table

he asks me my birthday

After a brief rundown of my zodiac sign and general personality

the pink faced mulatto mixed-breed old man

begins to read my story

like he's reading it from a book

Telling me that love is easier to find if you don't look

Suggesting that I slow down and take it easy on the road

He's right

because with two speeding tickets already in New York State

I don't have much left to go before I have to put on the brakes

Never looking up from the crumpled napkins, sesame seeds

and crumbs from hamburger rolls

he tells me that I'm too giving

and tend to fall in love with the wrong souls

Well that's true

But what does this wrinkled-ass man know about my life story?

Or is he reading my reactions to general statements

You know the ones that apply to everybody

but only seem to be meant for me

But while taking bites out of my Big Mac

I haven't taken my eyes off of him

He amazingly has not looked up once

After informing me of my love

and dedication to my mother and sister

he tells me that there are four women in my life

who profess their love

That's funny because there's only one that I really know of

But even then I'm doomed

So now I don't know who really loves me

and if they do, are they the right one?

I've been continuously watching my speedometer

making sure that I'm observing the posted speed limit

feeling guilty when I pass on the left

So, I sit behind the slow vehicles

wondering if one of those four women is driving in front of me

But I can't speed

So I will never be able to get next to her and see her face

And because I'm too giving

I set the clock in my car twenty minutes fast

So that if my passenger asks for the time

the answer that I give will only be a little bit correct

Therefore I'm only giving a little bit of myself

while maintaining the speed limit

and trying to keep up with the love of my life

The Poet

I am the poet

Speaker of the mind

Twisting the power of thought into words

My own literary masterpieces

created through your joys and pains

Interpreting your life through my eyes

A picture worth a thousand words

As you spill your guts – I listen

absorbing your sincerity and depicting it as senility

Literarily raping you of your innocence

Your story being placed among many in my little black book

Another notch in my pencil

because I've fucked your brains until you've cum

Your deepest and innermost thoughts are mine for the taking

And unless you read in between these lines

you'll never know that all this time

I was just faking

I am a poet

Possessing the ability to fantasize for those who can't

You give my poems to your lovers

and share tears

Leaving my pages damp

Expressing my political and social discontent

Analyzing and judging you

while I am yet to repent

Forging your experiences for my own deliriousness

An archeologist of mind and emotions

writing notes about the remains of your consciousness

I need you

Without you I am nothing

and have nothing without your emptiness and unhappiness

Without your joys and laughter

Because of your dependence on me

to verbalize what you want to see

I become on paper

the person you aim to be

I speak for you

and to you

I am the poet

We need each other

16 Shots to the Dome

41 shots in the frame of my door

as I explore the world of fear

Silver badges and black nines keep me in my place

While protective shields and teargas keep my people away

Sexually harassed

as they ram nightsticks up my ass

They call me Abner Diallo – the black man

With a pager in one hand

a bag of groceries in the other

I'm armed and dangerous

Public enemy number 1

5 – 0 said freeze

But instead they shot me 5 times in the back

labeling it as a random act

Charging me with resisting cardiac arrest

they appoint Ferguson as my public offender

We sit on the LIRR discussing ways to incriminate myself

in a system where you're judged by your color and gender

Black and man

I'm told to praise the red, white, and blue

So I spill my blood

Raise my white flag

waiting until the boys in blue put handcuffs on my black ass

I've seen horrors where words cannot express the pain

Cans of mace are emptied in my face

Unable to see clearly

badge numbers and license plates remain visions of a blur

They don't want me to see the truth

So they blind me

Leaving me with an inability

to experience this pain visually

Sirens blaring and clouding my brain

preventing me from hearing the words of their disdain

Hands cuffed to the middle of my buttocks

as if I were a slave waiting to be whipped

for disregarding the master's wish

If by chance I have the pleasure of a brief memory to treasure

a black night stick serves best to erase and delete

Swelling up my mouth

so I'm unable to speak

41 shots heard in the distance

Not necessarily black on black crime

or Bloods and Crips

Now I wonder what poor motherfucker was in the wrong place

at the wrong time

Not 4 thieving ass niggas taking his shit

but 4 of New York's Whitest emptying their clips

We no longer fear the thugs and black gangsters

But the slugs of pranksters who claim to protect us

Never did know that fecal matter could appear in a bladder

We've literally got this shit crossed

The sign didn't say "serve and protect"

it said "serve an ass whipping, neglect, and disrespect"

We've become dyslexic

Confusing acts of kindness with an urge to wreck shit

Now they change the venue of my rape case

or should I say the case of my rape

Taking me further upstate

Claiming to give the defendants a jury a peers

But instead they get 8 white racist motherfuckers

who've been practicing for years

4 sisters

who've probably received phone calls threatening their kids

and a media circus waiting to see these niggas flip

41 shots in the frame of my door

But this time I was prepared

Ducked behind the bag of groceries

Threw my pager on the floor

Cocked my shit

Raised my arm

Screamed out "REVOLUTION"

and let out 16 shots of my own

Facing Reality

Lying on my back

undead

Staring into my life

facing the realities that cause social casualties

Impressions on my pillow case and mattress

tell stories like chalk outlines

or the fossils found in igneous rocks on mountain tops

Dreams serving as my mind's defense

project my life in a false pretense

An afterlife which I have seen

before the first life sentence was complete

Experiencing my fantasies through the power of thought

while my fears remain afterthoughts

Recalling times when dreams have been confused with realities

and I woke up with all intentions of continuing where I left off

Not realizing that the interruption which I faced

was the sound of my alarm

Not just a break from the norm

I've seen the many faces that my mind is capable creating

Manipulating my ignorance

with the power of my own imagination

Through dreams I've seen life on the other side

took a turn for the worst

opened my eyes

and once again found myself revived

Bitch Ass Nigga

That ain't no "Bitch"

Nigga, look at that complexion

Hell yeah!

Right now you a nigga

'cuz

you showing that black woman the wrong kind of affection

She's stronger than you

lifted your spirits when they were down

mended your wounds when they were open

while her feet stayed planted firmly on the ground

That's your black woman

The mother of your earth

and through pain, blood, sweat, and tears

she's able to bring life

and willing to give birth

Risking her health and sacrificing her frame

Giving you a child

and willing to take your last name

Letting go of her individuality

Giving you unconditional love

and without hesitation you could strike her down

and make her a domestic casualty

Afraid because the man she trusted

shed her own blood

That ain't no "Bitch"

She's a black woman, mother to your earth

And without hesitation

you use her name in the same sentence as a curse

And as you struck her down with hate and malice

she forgave, made your food

and helped build your palace

But still you call her "Bitch"

Using your anger as your defense

Trying to hide your weaknesses

and rob that black woman of her strengths

Don't call that black woman a "Bitch"

The mother to your earth should be respected

And her strengths will allow your weaknesses

to be complimented

She'll love you as a black man

admire you as a friend

treasure you as a father

and value you as a husband

And then, you won't be that "nigga"

that you was in the beginning

Lunch with the Field Niggas

Here I come to the table

dressed in my clean clothes

Wearing my white pants

Smelling fresh like the flowers from the motherland

Place the napkin on my lap

'cuz that's where it's supposed to go

No dirt under my nails

'cuz inside Mr. Jackson lets us wash our hands with soap

They come up to eat

I seen them washing up

Using the same water that the cattle drink from

Their clothes still dusty from the fields

'cuz they couldn't shake it all off

They happy today

'cuz they get to eat before the dogs

Damn! They smell funny

Looking all tired and worn

Hands all torn up like they was playing in thorns

They not clean like me

Don't know what fork to use

or even where the napkin's supposed to be

Their clothes are older than mines

and some don't got no shoes

And lashings on their backs

But that's 'cuz they don't like to follow rules

Here comes Mr. Jackson

Everybody stands up when he comes around

And what's funny is when he talks

we all look down at our feet and the ground

We all say "Yessah"

Some say "Yes Massah"

But the ones from outside usually say it faster

I guess we not really different

Except our clothes are cleaner than theirs

But when Mr. Jackson comes around

I think we all get a little scared

The Life You Take

You take this life and don't even think

Does it know what's going on?

Or did it have any say in its own destiny

Does it want a chance to be born?

Were those really your tears in the sink?

Was the dream you had its dream or your own?

Is it scared because you're scared?

Alone because you're alone?

Is it a conscious being?

Able to feel pain?

Could it cry out for help?

Does it know you haven't given it a name?

Can it hear your words,

understand your thoughts

and feel your emotions?

Does it know why its life is so controversial?

Realize that it's caused so much commotion?

You take this life and don't even think

maybe this life that you take is already able to think

Nigger (nig'er)

They call me "nigger"

Renamed my whole race

Even put it in the book of words

Right after "niggardly" and when spelled phonetically

comes damned close to an African place

I call them "cowards"

Afraid to face the truth

because this nigger built the earth

and watered the grass when it was just roots.

Afraid, so you call me "nigger"

and "nig-ate" everything black

because you know that a drop of our soul

could totally change your genetic track

Making you more beautiful than nine months before

Making you stronger than the chains that we once wore

Your women love our men

The pride, innocence and the powerful presence

Your men love our women

The strength, sexuality and the motherly essence

So you hide that love

Shade it with hate

Replace it with fear

You created the "nigger"

supported by facts and rates

Give it poor housing

Education

Healthcare

Welfare

No job

No chance

"No service for niggers here"

You created the "nigger"

Built it up in your mind

of how we spit fire, practiced voodoo and cast spells

Featuring us in the circus of media

Forcing us to fear ourselves

Treating us like freak shows

Praising us for our physical strengths

Claiming our intellectual inferiority

Overlooking the milestones we set and things we invent

You created the "nigger"

Ignorant to the facts

But now we ain't niggers

We just plain old black

Pocahontas

Chinky-eyed shorty

with soft wavy hair down to her ass

Not exactly black

But damn far from white

Dark enough so that I ain't crossing over

But light enough that I can see her at night

I call her China, Asia, Japan, Taiwan

Half-black

Her mother's Cherokee mixed with Aborigine

and her father's from the Sudan

She got an accent too – I think it's from England

Matter of fact

She said that her great grandfather was born in Kingston

So I guess that technically makes her part Jamaican

She's 21

Born in Brooklyn

Moved to PG when she was 3

That's in Maryland

where all the high-class half-blacks with the high-ends be

She got light eyes

One's light brown and the other is gray

She's smart and she got doe

Stripper by night and student by day

Her peeps got her a crib in the white part of DC

About to graduate from Georgetown

with a degree in African-American Psychology

a minor in Criminal Justice

She also dances

and wants to be in videos for the music industry

or a host of a rap video show on BET

Struggle for Life

Struggling to catch a breath like a person drowning at the beach

after being pulled in by the undertow

Holding on for dear life

as if I'm a child who accidentally climbed out

onto the ledge of a window

Screaming and crying for my mother who's sleeping

My voice drowned out by the TV blasting in the backroom

Tears flowing down my face from the thought of letting go

Realizing that my screams are in vein

because the only people that hear are the ones down below...

They just want to see me jump

I want to pull myself to safety

But I'm tired

only strong enough to hold the weight of my frail body

for short periods of time

The hope and love of life which I have experienced until now

has given me the strength to hold on this long

In a flash I teleport

Now finding myself trying to walk a straight path

Aware of the obstacles which I will encounter on the way

But with every path I choose I am confronted

with seventy mile an hour winds against my chest

Leaning forward I struggle and reach for poles to grab

so that I have the opportunity to take a rest.

But the poles embedded two feet into the ground

are less stable than my own body weight

Exhausted, I turn around ready to give up

But the wind is still blowing against my face

It's just as hard to go back as it is to go forward

Figuring that choosing another path will solve my problems

I look to the left

Again met by the force of the wind

Looking to the right I see the reflection of my dark complexion

realizing that the root of my problems just might be my skin

and before the wind can hit me I teleport again

Jumping from struggle to struggle

Nothing's easy in this world

That's what my father told me

And in my pain and frustration there's no one to help

No one to give me words of wisdom or cheers of support

So all I can do is teleport

Real Nigga

Come on money

You gonna bust me because of a stare

or some shit you want of mine.

Taking my life over some bullshit

Like I really have time to be sittin' up in a hospital

with a bullet in my spine

Fuck yeah!

You gonna have to shoot me in the back

because I'ma run like hell

You can call me a bitch

But I guess you the real nigga

holding full clips

Drop that heat money

Ball your fists

Send me to the hospital for a broken nose

not because I failed to wear a vest under my clothes

Call yourself the man

because you pull out your heat

unlock the safety

and leave a slug in my ass from a distance of 100 feet

Meanwhile

to see Mike Tyson knocking niggas out with one blow

you'll pay 50 dollars for pay per view

and charge your peeps 10 a head

Sucking his dick with every punch he throws

And when it's over he's "the fuckin' man"

That nigga gets paid 4 million

for a minute and a half of his time

And you're gonna risk facing 25 to life for taking mine.

If you think I'm worth that much go ahead real nigga

Pull that steel trigger

Take the sixty dollars from my pocket

and treat yourself to a value meal a day for the next two weeks

Or better yet, buy a pack of cigarettes

and save the change to start up your commissary

Open Your Eyes, See What I See

With a soul as strong as an arc

withstanding forty days and forty nights

of torrential tribulations

You appear unharmed

unaffected by what you have encountered

You have single handedly battled an army

of frustrating deception

Growing from your past

you have turned the outlook of your future

into something glorious

Uncovering the ability to smile through your tears

I see strength in your weakness

I see strength in your fears

Refusing to allow gravity to pull you down

you continue to climb

refusing to rest in between time

I watch you

pausing between breaths to regain your continuousness

Glossy-eyed

fighting the tears from reaching your cheeks

But on the inside you cry harder than words can describe

But that doesn't make you weak

I see strength in your fears

Strength that has grown over years

while you have not realized what has made you who you are

You have grown from your mistakes

Experience has helped to solidify your frame

Your shell is the only thing that can be broken

But your soul is what restores it to its original shape

I see strength

Open your eyes...see what I see

Part 2: Love (lŭv)

1: A strong affection for or attachment to another person based on regard or shared experiences or interests.[2]

2: A zero score in tennis[3]

3: freaking emotions; something having to do with me liking her, a lot more than "like," and the things I'm willing to do to show it.

Dying For Your Love

I've died twice today

Once when I hurt you

and then when I saw you cry

When you dropped to the ground

my heart fell twice as fast

I wanted to hold you up

But the weight of your sorrow

your body and my guilt

was too much for me to carry alone

I needed you to help

Just like you've been there to help me before

But I've torn away at your trust

and scarred the love that you have for me

I don't know if you're willing to help me anymore

But if you are

I'm falling

with all of this weight on my shoulders

And even though I've caused us both to fall

I can't hold us up alone

I'm not strong enough

You've been my inspiration

and my adrenaline

I need a push

I need you to resuscitate me

Bring me back to life

So that my heart can start pumping

and I can find the strength to keep us from hitting the ground

This is a hard fall

So I'm gonna put my hand out

and grab hold of the closest thing

and with your hand in my other

I'll swing you to safety

If I miss

I'll put my hand in front of me

Still holding you in my other arm

Break our fall

So that we can get up and walk again

Don't Let Go

Don't let go baby

I've got an entire life to live, worlds to explore,

and people to see

I've got smiles to smile

heights to reach

love to give

places to be

I've made mistakes

Are they unforgivable?

Surpassing the ability to be forgotten?

Overshadowing the times I've put smiles on your face,

disrupting the flow of tears

leaving no place for a frown to set?

Are they unbearable?

Stronger than a love that has withstood erosion

caused by time and the forces of mother nature?

A love seamless in its design and having no definite foundation

Breathing and living off of what was meant

Unimaginable in my mind

and emotionally unparalleled to any dream I've dreamt

Don't let go baby

You have an entire life to live

worlds to explore

and people to see

You've got smiles to smile

heights to reach

love to give

places to be

You've got me

I've been here throughout your life

Passing by

Fulfilling your unexpected dreams

Waiting for the right time to pop into your mind

Holding out for the perfect moment to fulfill your needs

Don't let my faults and imperfections blind you

making you incapable of seeing my qualities

Our paths etched in stone like a bible of destiny

For our child may be the savior of the Savior

The anti Anti-Christ

Or maybe we can just share the joy of our ability to create a life

Don't let go baby

We have an entire life to live

worlds to explore

and people to see

We've got smiles to smile

heights to reach

love to give

places to be

We can't let our mistakes and misunderstandings

disrupt this flow

allowing something destined for near perfection

to be controlled by our egos

I'm on my hands and knees

Using elbows and some grease

Holding on for dear life as if I don't have the option to release

I ain't letting go baby

I have my life to give you

and a world too

I've got people to see

I have to tell them how much I love you

My Love

My love

I've spent my life living for you

Passed you in my dreams

and my reality

I've felt fear

and have been given strength through your courage

You have helped me realize who I am

and what I need to do

Everything good that I do

I do for you

While my mistakes and faults

stem from the selfishness of my thoughts

My heart controlling my emotions

can only make mere suggestions to my mind

But it is there that my actions

and my reactions are decided

Take my hand and lead me

I am lost in my own insecurities

Help me find the connection between heart and mind

where reason and life truly begin

and a bond that is created through adoration

I've spent my life living for you

Try to live for me

Understand that I am fallible

But also know that I am malleable

and with each misstep that I take

I need your help

I need your strength

to help me step in the right place

Weight of Love

You have kept me grounded

Holding me down

when other things have tried to drag me away

and now you're letting go

I feel as if I'm too light

like something is lifting me off of the ground

You've been my anchor

keeping me stable and bound

While the winds have blown across my troubled path

your love has saved me

like boarded up windows in a hurricane

And as we both sit here

knees to our chest

and tears running down our faces

I know that it's you I want to spend my life with

My heart beginning to defy gravity

The feeling of an empty world without you

I'm floating away

leaving behind everything that I know

Hold me

I'm lifting off of the love that has been my foundation

A love that has kept me secure in what I thought were restraints

You've set me free

but I'm afraid

The wind is too strong for my fragile wings

I want to be safe

Back in my cage

where I know I'll be fed everyday

I know you'll walk by and wave my way

I love you

All this time I thought I wanted to be free

I just wanted to see what it would be like if you didn't hold me

War

My desire to make you smile has backfired

leaving shrapnel in my eyes

Now what once housed a vision filled with love

only brings fears of loneliness

Showering love letters with tears

Now wars are waged

My mind desperately trying to protect itself against

the attacks of my heart

My heart depriving my brain of oxygen

in attempts to weaken its powers of rational thinking

I don't want to hear your voice

But yet I do want to hear from you

Wondering if you care has got me playing Russian roulette

...with my phone

Putting the ear piece to my head

 and waiting for the pain of a single tone

Could you really not care?

Not a message confirming your love

Fuck You!

That's all I can say before the actual pain sets in

Slowly my body falls to the floor

My heart's tactics of deprivation are successful

Sending me into a sleep

only to be interrupted by your phone call

Either that or the sound of my alarm

Fuck You!

I'm right, you're wrong

Or could it be an air raid

Angry words flying through the sky

destroying all that exists

While your front line clears out all signs of life

Throwing grenades in the tunnels of my ears

All I hear is shouts and screams

I'm losing the war

You're killing me

My attempts of retaliation being destroyed

by landmines and booby traps

My words are like six shooters

Yours are like gats

Leaving holes in my reasons like snipers in tall grasses

waiting for me to pop my head into your line of fire

But my troops have a desire

We shall overcome some day...

Someday

Standing our ground and holding it down

Our fighter pilots found a way to drop napalm on the ground

But as quickly as that occurs

It begins to rain

You shoot down my planes

Once again all my hopes and dreams washed down the drain

Finally, making a hard decision to accept defeat

RETREAT!!

I stop, drop and roll

It's time to bail

Staying low and avoiding the smoke

because I never inhale

What is "It"?

I don't know what "it" is

As powerful as "it" chooses to be

"It" could be the sound of your voice for him

or the way you smell for me

"It's" the last thing on my mind before I go to sleep

the first thing in the beginning of my week

"It's" peaceful

Soothing as the sound of rain landing on the leaves of trees

Frustrated at the mystery of what "it" is

I find myself staring at nothing

except for the way I think "it" appears

But does "it" exist?

Or is "it" my imagination

constantly conjuring up figments of ecstasy

Blessing me with unfamiliar visions

"It" is growing inside of me

Becoming stronger as the days grow shorter

"It" seems to predict my actions

and control my intentions

"It" is the color of everything that makes me smile

and the smell of your perfume in the air

Unsure of what "it" is

I search an endless search

Waiting until "it" presents itself

And "it" did

In the form of what I wished "it" to be

and all that I am able to see

There "it" was standing right in front of me

"It" was everywhere and everything

Perfect to me, as "it" appears perfect to him

What is "it" that you do?

Because I'm overwhelmed by the thought of you

Our most joyous moments are ineffable

leaving me pondering if "it" is natural

Is this how "it" is supposed to be?

Or is "it" just love in "its" highest degree

Nerves

Your lips, your face,

Your perfect embrace – holding me

like you're just trying to keep me safe.

Your love constantly in sync with mine

I can see it in your eyes

Taste it on your lips

And feel it between your thighs

You got some motherfuckin' nerves!

Making it feel like this

Exploring my soul with your fingertips

The taste of your love resting

so, so easily on the tip of my tongue

Your eyes caressing my soul –

Telling me when to rise

Praying that I don't have to let go

You got some motherfuckin' nerves!

Asking me how it feels

Making me want to call your name

Fighting with my ego to just let go

But being a man – they don't want me to let you know

I'm not supposed to tell you about the warmth I feel when

your love touches the tip of my soul

Warming it where it was once cold

You got some motherfuckin' nerves!

Placing my soul inside of your love

Your eyes caressing my eyes

while I'm thanking you for making me rise

Needing to call out your name

Happy that I used the Lord's in vein

Burying my face in the cusp of your neck

Trying to figure out how your own warmth

made you so wet

You got some motherfuckin' nerves!

Making my soul feel so good

Allowing your love to keep it so warm

Allowing your eyes to caress it and make me rise

Oh God – it feels so good when it's inside

You got some motherfuckin' nerves!

Makin' it feel like this

Askin' me how it feels

Placing my soul inside of your love

Makin' my soul feel so good

Makin' me use my Lord's name in vein

Ohhh Baby – Makin' me call out your name

Black-Eyed Peas & Cornbread

I've tasted love

Had a full plate that I couldn't get enough of

Cleaned it dry

Even cracked the chicken leg and ate the marrow inside

Unbuttoned my pants when I was done

Stretched

Adjusted my position

Leaned back and began nodding my head

That shit was good!

but then came the black-eyed peas and cornbread

I thought I had tasted love

I didn't know there was more to the meal

So there I sat

licking my lips

with a grin on my face

wondering how you managed to make it so great

I've had black-eyed peas

But yours seem to melt in my mouth

And your cornbread

makes me wanna' move down south

get me a plate and fill it 'til it spills over the sides

sitting there with a mouth full of black-eyed

I've tasted love

Not what I tasted before

This love I've tasted got something more

A little bit of spice

Or maybe it's just the pot it was in

I'm trying to get more if there's anything left

From what I see

you could cook a whole batch just for me

I won't waste it or throw it away

I'll wrap it up tight

and save it for another day

or maybe I'll loosen my belt

adjust my position

and dig on in

Brown Eyes

Brown eyes, staring into my soul

Caught a peek at my hand

Knowing that I'm gonna fold

Ain't give me a chance to say a motherfuckin' word

Shit!

A booty like that

made my neck snap

Damn!

Are my words startin' to slur?

I can't even see clearly now

Were we talkin' about the Knicks or . . .

Excuse me, can I have another drink?

Oh, I asked already?

My bad

Brown eyes, running through my mind

Shhhh...I'm trying to think.

Can I take you to dinner or get you another drink?

Why am I staring at you like that?

Well, because I'm afraid to blink.

Your brown eyes got me hypnotized

Afraid that you'll be gone when I open my eyes

Taking everything but the visions of your face

and of course the kitchen sink

Brown eyes, I hope you don't mind if I stare

I'm afraid to blink.

I see a future for the two of us

And I'm afraid that if I close my eyes,

it might disappear.

De ja` vu

Is it me?

or is this all too familiar?

I seem to recall this whole scene

And your smile is in my mind

clear as a picture

I swear I've had these same thoughts

heard the same nouns, adjectives, and verbs

How could I forget your lips?

The way they caress your every word

This shit got me buggin'

Clear to me as if it just happened

Remembering the way you moved

down to the way you were laughing

Loving every moment now

knowing that it's worth repeating

Forecasting your next sentence

as if my satellites circled the map of your brain

Sending me back visuals of your patterns

predictions that Dionne and her friends couldn't fathom

and knowledge that only gods from above could explain

Right now I know you

Better than you know yourself

I was given a glimpse of our future

the ability to alter our destiny

temporarily displace time

and change something that was meant to be

Just this moment

I've used another one percent of my mental capacity

Experienced a surge in my Energizer battery

causing me to flash back and forth

between what is and what could be reality

Dreams

Secretly I dream of Genie

Granting me wishes of eating cherries

on the sun beaten paths of your valleys

Praising Venus and Aphrodite

for taste buds

and the ability to make rivers flow

where land was once dehydrating

Passing time while blowing your mind

with tongue lashes that give you whip lash

Hiding my face in between your thighs

like a child hides his face when surprised

Secretly I dream of Genie

Granting me wishes of eating giant chocolate kisses

Licking them from the base

and slowly sucking on the tips

Melts in my mouth

Not in my hands

Praising Venus and Aphrodite

for their ability to make mountains out of molehills

woman out of man

Hardened nipples

sensitive to warm touches of my lips

on "caramelled," sun scorched skin

laced with marks of passion

and remembrance of what had been

Secretly I dream of Genie

Granting me wishes

Deep breaths of life

as your chest rises and falls

Hands, lips, tongue

Exploring your every things

Your alls

Expressing affection

through injections from erections

leaving impressions

in the imperfections of your perfection

Endless Beginnings

Unable to see clearly

I imagine

in a distant future

a fallacy

Envisioning a you and I

that cannot exist alongside real ty

Destiny won't allow us to cross physical paths

So we are subjected to the torture of thoughts and voice

while reasoning has no place

A love bound by itself

Bound by a truth of what must not be

Separated by the distance

of our deepest thoughts

and intimacies that only dream to exist

I fantasize of becoming delusional

Enough to make this illusion tangible in my mind

But to miss you is to realize

that this illusion is the result of being blind

Blinded by hopeless attempts at a glimpse of this fantasy

Wondering if there will be a next lifetime

where this infinite road taken by our souls

allows us to experience togetherness

Futile attempts at experiencing love

has us driving down a two way street

only to pass each other by

As I look back to shout

The hands of time grab me

Pulling me away as I experience spasms

and mental orgasms

from envisioning and you and I

that should have never been fathomed

Intrigue

Intrigued by the fact that I know nothing

I only see your beauty and the little bit of "you" that you share

But behind that picture lies a thousand words

encrypted by shadows of a doubt

Lover by day, I'm lost in a fantasy

imagining what your nights could be about

Whispering secrets in my ear

Letting me in on your every hope and desire

but they are too low for me to actually hear

Loving the mystery of what could be

A romance novel where pages are blank

with no beginning and no end

There's more to you

hidden behind suggestive smiles and subtle hints

Moments where thoughts of wet kisses remain thoughts

imprinting the mellifluous taste of your love on my lips

Caressing the idea of holding you in my arms

Filling my emptiness with the weight of your charms

Day dreaming of kisses on my pelvic bone

that leave me inebriated

High from the feeling of not being alone

Timeless

Our love knows no time

And if it did you'd have no doubts

These 3 years, 4 months, 21days,

14 hours, 8 minutes, and 38 seconds

could tell all what love is about.

And if it knew time it'd be mad as hell

The way we've spent time, used time,

wasted time, forgot about time,

taking it for granted

assuming we've used it well.

This love don't know a thing about time

Or else I wouldn't have had the desire to spend my life with you

The first time I felt its power,

The first time I let you know

and every time I saw your face

knowing the word "Love" will follow.

Our love knows no time

But they tell me to slow down

You're moving too quick

Take your time

You don't want to get whipped

You ain't been together long enough

to be talking about no marriage

But yet they all surprised

because we ain't pushing no carriage.

Our love knows no time

It only knows the love we have

It knows the joy that you bring me

and how complete we are together

Our love knows no time

It only knows what it sees

That you and I are its creators

and something meant to be.

Love Me

Why do you make it so hard to love you?

Making it so difficult to complete this picture

A masterpiece without a frame

almost as priceless as the theme

Let me love you the way you deserve to be

without depriving yourself of the love I'm capable of giving

Pushing me away with every smile

willing to forget the importance of time

Will yourself the strength to accept all that this love can offer

and leave yourself open to the joy and emotion that it can bring

I feel alone

Experiencing a passion created to be shared

Don't make me feel as if I'm crazy to love you the way that I do

Don't punish me for my willingness to sacrifice

or my willingness to care

Give to me what you are able to give

Let me feel the way I think I make you feel

Don't allow your independence

to suffocate the joys of codependence

A feeling of needing because you want to need

Allow loving me to overwhelm you

rendering you motionless in my arms

instead of subjecting me to your emotionless charms

Love me the way that you know I should be

the way you wish to be loved

You have something with me that so many desire

Cherish it, nurture it, respect it

Because it can't grow on its own

Memories of You

Memories of you

Always dwelling in my mind

Causing me to forget the reasons

why people keep track of time

If the days never began and nights would never end

then I could watch the universe in your eyes

from its beginning, to its end.

If only memories of you

would leave my mind

I could breathe without missing your voice

I could smile without you being the cause

And wouldn't know the feeling

of having you in my life.

But memories of you are always on my mind

Therefore I suffer with the time we don't share

and feel pain when the morning comes

I have to continue breathing when you're not there

And know what it is to be in love

I know of sleepless nights when I've done wrong

And sleepless nights figuring how to do right

Memories of you

Keep me looking forward to the next day

And let me dream of all great things

Let me smile when I'm alone

And appreciate the joy this love brings

Memories of you keep me alive

when there is no reason to be

I often wonder if you have memories of me

A Moment's Notice

Sometimes I get the urge to tell you "I love you"

just because if feels right

Unknowing of the possibility that these feelings actually exist

or maybe the words just fit perfectly into this moment

Like when I stare into your eyes

the reflections from the candle light seem to be dancing

I still treasure it

Bathing my soul in our happiness

A moment full of bliss

soon to be forgotten by what tomorrow brings

My heart sings aloud

Racing with every thought of your lips against my own

Our touches celebrating this picture's physical form

Right now you're my earth

My last thought until the next one intervenes

Imposing on my short fantasies and stories

serving as distractions from my peace

Had I the ability to freeze time

I could enjoy a moment for all that it's worth

Reliving it infinitely in my mind.

Appreciating the repetitiveness

like I'm watching the same scene in a movie

But this time I notice its differerces

Still smiling

Heart still racing

The moment hasn't changed

It's just a different day

Hair pulled back

You're dressed in different clothes

No flickering candles

No thoughts to impose

The only thing is I still see the same face

but haven't lost the urge to say what I wanted to say yesterday

Beyond

I've experienced love

But sometimes you get that feeling

when the word LOVE is just not enough

When you've entered a level unfamiliar to common ground

Knowing that what you feel is stronger than the highest sound

Shattering glass if it is ever fully expressed

It is something more

Something that I am afraid to endure

Like traveling a foreign path

Unpaved

Still fresh with tall grass

I've found love beyond love

Spent an endless search to find the perfect word

But none qualify

No word can truly exemplify

And as rain drops land on my brow

I'm reminded of what this feeling is about

It's gone beyond love

Built a world of its own in my chest

Taken over my heart

Leaving me completely speechless

Overwhelming thoughts of you flood my mind

as I'm emotionally overtaken by thoughts of time

On this fresh path I try to maintain its purity

Carefully moving leaves and branches

without scarring its beauty

I'm in love

Or something more than that

I'm beyond love

Imagining bathing you in the tears of my joy

Yes I cry

Deep inside

when I think of not having you by my side

I walk this path...stepping over the grass

waiting to trip and fall into your arms

But you doubt my sincerity

and question my ability to love beyond love

I've asked the powers that be to free me

Release me from this endless pain

I've loved you more than you can fathom

Now let me go

Tell me that your love is not that same

Part 3: The Words (da wûrdz)

1: A discourse or talk: SPEECH.[4]

2: the expressed or manifested mind and will of God[5]

3: some shit on my mind that I decided to write, but never had enough to write a full book about.

New York's Finest

The bruises were there for over a week. Only sixteen years old, I would stare at them like a new tattoo or tribal marks signifying a rite of passage; sort of a "black Bar Mitzvah," representing childlike innocence being evicted by grown man experience, instead of a celebratory religious occasion. I imagined the shackles of slaves raised above stretched bodies, whipped with stinging exposed burning skin and torn flesh. I saw black castrated men, boys, children, raped and beaten women, tied to rope, and being dragged down dark dirt country roads by pickup trucks filled with cackling white men jeering and cheering. I connected the little red blood clotted dots that circled both wrists, forming the words, "LET MY PEOPLE GO."

I sat looking in disbelief at two of my friends being dragged off the Q30 bus, not understanding how shooting water out of a bus window could cause the NYPD to react the way that they did. Even more puzzling was one of New York's finest running up on me like a linebacker sacking a quarterback, and snatching my all black AK-47 replica water gun out of my hands. Yes it was black, but the most damage that it could have caused was a wet t-shirt and a bunch of soaked-ass kids. When I stood up to defend my honor, the boy in blue threatened me with a few simple words; "Do you want me to take you in too?" So, there I stood with the rest of the "niggers" who were bused in from South Jamaica, Queens to attend the less ethnically balanced Francis Lewis H.S., shouting and pleading for them to "let my people go." I guess I got off easy. He could of easily have shot me claiming to have heard a gun-shot fired from my direction. Black water guns, wallets, loaves of bread, and hair brushes have one thing in common; they are all dangerous in the hands of black men.

From the conversation overheard between a few of the police officers, I came to the conclusion that my friends fit the description; black males, young to old, breathing, and most likely in the state of New York. While apprehending my friends, the nation's biggest group of donut consumers forgot to inform them of their Miranda Rights; a rule which many state and local governments continue to debate over its necessity during the arrest process. Being that we are arrested on a daily basis, there's no need for them to keep repeating themselves. After "macing" our savaged asses in this period of civil unrest, they drove off with my friends in the back of their squad car. As I watched what was already a blur become even blurrier, tears poured from my eyes. Not from pain, agony, or disappointment, but mace is no bullshit. Still not completely understanding what had just occurred, I sat in the back of the bus silent, confused, and frustrated with the afternoon's events. I went home and said nothing. I never mentioned my experience to either of my parents. I absorbed it and accepted it as a cultural and racially distributed sedative.

The night they were arrested my friends were released under their parents' custody and held out of school until the entire situation was cleared up. The next day, there were detectives at Francis Lewis high school confirming with the principal the whereabouts of my two friends. Ironically, the both of them were in his office during the time of the actual crime for doing something else that was disruptive to the academic flow of our fine educational establishment. Rumors travelled throughout the school campus, but we never found out what crime was committed and why our bus was pulled over. Our friends simply returned to school without comment or protest. It was as if they were taken by aliens, probed, studied, and returned to the point of abduction; memories wiped clean and no recollection of how they obtained the bruises on their wrists or the soreness in their shoulders.

Occasionally, we would see the police officers who pulled my friends off the bus. They would ask if we were staying out of trouble, slowly driving beside us as we walked to the bus stop or the school. Partially ignoring us, they would do this until they received another more urgent call on the radio. It was reminiscent of the Civil Rights era when young black men and women would be followed for miles as police officers antagonized them, waiting for an opportunity to throw them in jail, hose them down, or release a vicious German Sheppard who already became fond of the taste of dark flesh. Our answers were always short and direct, straight and to the point, vague, cold, and evasive, but hidden within those answers were hints of "mind your fucking business" and "get off my damn back."

That being my first direct encounter with the NYPD, was what formed the bitter taste in my mouth that exists to this present day. As I continued to experience, witness, or hear about other incidents involving the police, my disdain for them increased. Throughout my tenure at Francis Lewis High School, I would be subjected to several after-basketball practice searches. The kind where the first question is, "what are you doing around here so late?" followed by "what school?" and then "pick up your shit and go home." Of course this was after they emptied the contents from my book bag and duffle bag on the sidewalk, patted me down, went through my pockets and removed me from the hood of their car. Many of us were thrown in the back of police cars while they radioed in to the precinct, ran through police reports and profiles hoping that one of us would be lucky enough to fit a description. We were never so lucky.

By the eleventh grade, the sight of the NYPD infuriated me instead of eliciting fear. Just the mere thought of what they had done to my friends and I sparked a raging fire within. We would challenge them with ice cold stares, daring them to fuck with us. When confronted, we reminded them of our right to free speech, our ability to assemble freely, requested warrants, and referenced Rodney King or other similar situations. I recall standing amidst crowds of teenagers yelling, "Fuck the Police!" as they drove by. The revolution was not televised, but the movement had begun.

It was and still is almost impossible for Black and Hispanic, youth and old alike to respect the New York Police Department, any police department for that matter. Surrounded by eight police cars, blaring sirens, flashing lights, and raised guns, an old college girlfriend was stripped of her leather jacket in the dead of winter after someone reported being mugged. After the store where I worked was robbed, my boss boosted me up to a window so that I could climb out, run next door, and report the robbery. I stood outside in the cold for twenty minutes waiting for the police, who when arrived, threw me against a police car, searched me for weapons, and questioned me until they were able to kick down the door and let my boss out to vouch for me. There's just no way. We've been victims of way too many instances of unnecessary suspicion, brutality, roughness, and harassment. I've seen too many of my brothers' skulls smashed in by the night-sticks of both black and white cops who simply feel the need to express their power through force.

I've seen horrors during my years. I've seen faces that resemble my own covered with blood and tears; bodies riddled with bullets. On one occasion a few police grabbed one of my friends off the street after allowing a victim of an armed robbery to point him out of a group of ten or so black teens standing on a corner. It was nineteen ninety two and the description was a young black male, fifteen to thirty-five, five feet to six feet, with an army fatigue jacket. Now, if you didn't know or just happened to be suffering from a case of temporary amnesia, everybody and their grandfather owned an army fatigue jacket. After throwing him to the ground and applying about four hundred pounds of pressure to his back, my friend was thrown in jail for the weekend. Having to re-mortgage their house and borrow from friends and family, his parents finally gathered up the money to bail him out. They drove themselves deeper into debt while accumulating an abundance of legal fees. After months of court appearances, all of the charges were dropped as the victims were coerced by the police into pointing out my friend that night, nor did they actually remember what the suspect looked like, except of course for the fact that he was a nigger with an army jacket. That's all it took to fuck up his life.

In addition to New Jersey Turnpike profiling and routine check-points throughout New York City and Nassau County, a minority male can't safely drive a nice car or any vehicle with rims or tinted windows without being followed and eventually stopped. During the short period of time that I had rims on my car in nineteen ninety nine, I received more tickets for bullshit laws and violations than I had in all of the years that I had a drivers' license. I worried more about being stopped and harassed by police than being car jacked or getting into a car accident. I eventually took the flashy wheels off and returned my car to its original manufactured appearance. I guess the assumption is that if you're a minority with a halfway decent car, then you obviously did something illegal to get it and you're probably continuing those same activities in order to keep it.

I wasn't always old enough or mature enough to realize what I was going to experience for the rest of my life. I didn't completely understand that my color would cause such a national, social, political, and multi-dimensional uproar. Although I always found myself relating more to the image of Malcolm X staring out of his window with his assault rifle, I was also taught about Martin Luther King, Jr. and his peaceful strides; his marches, speeches, and Rosa Parks' refusal to get up from her seat or off the bus. I recognized the struggles that existed, but for all intended purposes I thought we had overcome. At least that's what they taught me. My parents subtly informed me of the continued oppression and racism that existed. My father taught me to stand up for myself in the face of any form of oppression, personal, social, financial. But while growing up playing "cops and robbers", the boys in blue were the good guys. They arrested people whether they were White, Black, or Hispanic. Bruce Lee got chased all over the place for kickin' ass. Shaft was just a bad motherfucker. The Dukes of Hazard were always speeding and shit. Cheech and Chong smoked until their lungs grew its own weed. Things just seemed fair back then.

We seem to continue down the same road year after year. Stay out of the way and out of trouble. The fact that statistically I am supposed to be in jail or dead, irresponsibly fathering children, who I am not going to acknowledge or take care of, is another twist of lemon in the already bitter tasting glass of reality. If by chance I take all necessary steps, every alternative path, make all the right decisions, and manage to avoid confrontation or situations that will place me in the face of the law, I am still likely to be victimized by a decrepit law enforcement system that has a lengthy history of abuse, especially when dealing with Black and Hispanic men. All I can do is stand my ground and prepare for the worst. I know that not all police officers fall into this category, but in my experiences, I haven't met enough of them. My vote: Majority rules. I note to myself, "he was pretty nice," and as they politely hand me a speeding ticket or pull me over inquiring whether or not I am lost, I thank them for choosing me. But I cautiously breathe a sigh of relief as they speed off; neither me or my passenger harmed; no bruises on my wrists from tightly applied handcuffs; no mace, no guns drawn, no piss in my pants, no lawyers, no "Fuck The Police" signs, no Al Sharpton or marches down Linden Boulevard; just me, my speeding ticket, and my experiences.

Diallo's Fury

Since the killing of Amadou Diallo (February 1999) when I wrote this, through November 2007, there continues to be killings at the hands of the New York City Police Department. Not counting the instances of police brutality and abuse of authority that have not resulted in a death, in New York alone, the climate between the people and the police still remains one that is laden with mistrust and resentment...a continually growing divide between the citizens and those entrusted to protect them. Sadly nothing has changed except for the administration. Even the governors of cities and states that do see a problem endure political arm-wrestling with police commissioners and supporters who have covered up these injustices. Not forgetting the fact that at times police officers are faced with challenging and life threatening situations, too often their resolutions for minor and major situations alike are acts of unnecessary force and unjustified procedures that only lead us to pose the question... "When does it stop?"

41 shots rang out. 19 of which lifted Amadou Diallo off of the ground. As he lay in a pool of his own blood, his soul knew there would be justice. Upon breaking the news of her son's death to his mother, her screams of his name "Amadou!" shattered the hearts of many throughout the world. Bringing forth the reality that a black man's life is as worthless to some as it was when we were first kidnapped from our land some 400 years ago. "41 shots" is all I can think of as I imagine four of NYPD's bravest firing at a man because they "thought." But the reality is that as police officers, they are invincible; unable to be viewed by a court of law and blessed with the presumption that because they are New York's Finest, they are unable to do wrong. The wrongs that they do are excusable and understandable. I knew in my heart that they would not escape God's wrath or the laws of common sense.

Common sense allows a person to know right from wrong without the need for much evidence and proof of fault. Common sense allows me to see that 41 shots is not a reaction to someone putting his keys in the door of his home, but evidence of the cruelty and hate that existed and grew within these four men. 19 shots lifted a man up to his savior who himself could not predict his son's fate. A fate that occurred because of his hopes of making it in the big city. He made it. Diallo made it big. The newspapers and magazines were emblazoned with his last name for over a year. Common sense should have been the decision-maker.

All I envision are white people throughout the nation sitting at their dinner tables with their plaid shirts and dungarees, some putting down their golf clubs, and others standing at their sinks washing the grease brought home from the mechanic shops. Many of them saying to their families, "that nigger should have stayed his ass in Africa." Not all, but some. And as their young children hear that discussion, they themselves begin to acquire the hate and anger toward us. Not all, but some. I also think how Africans, West Indians, and other immigrants of color will come to these great states knowing of this situation, but assuming it was just isolated to one person. Is it? Part of me died.

February 25, 2000 is when I saw the turn of the millennium and a new reality for minorities. Four police officers charged with four counts of murder, negligent homicide, second degree murder, and all types of other shit for shooting Amadou Diallo on the steps

83

of his home because he appeared to be suspicious, were acquitted of all charges. Boss, Carroll, McMellon, and Murphy all escaped punishment because they are white and Diallo was black. They are cops and he was not. As far as the authorities are concerned, we are always suspicious. So shooting us on the steps of our homes is now permissible in the court of law. Unable to ever imagine a situation similar to the Rodney King beating, verdict, and the riots that broke out as a result, I had no idea that it could occur again. Especially in a city as culturally diverse as New York.

I'm left nearly speechless. All I can do is sit frozen at my desk unable to exchange words with my white supervisor sitting on the other side of the office. Not knowing if he agrees with the verdict, knows of the verdict, or even cares about the outcome. Afraid that the wrong word from him could cause me to flip out and bash his head in with my computer monitor. Because although I am tolerant, I believe that I am still holding a lot of anger inside and waiting for a chance to release the pressure that has built up for over 22 years; since that little white boy called me "blue" in kinder garden, since that Chinese kid called me a "nigger" in high school, or since a white co-worker at my job jokingly referred to the jeans, t-shirt, and construction boots that I wore on a Summer Friday as "gangsta rap clothing." As my chest throbs from the pain of my heart's attempts to explode, my stomach boils with the intensity of a sweltering sun beating down on the backs on my enslaved ancestors. Scars are beginning to swell, bearing the pain of fresh lashings from the whip of a slave master. Blood throbs and slams against the inside of my skull, resembling the muffled screams of a woman being raped and threatened by a white slave owner promising to sell off her children if she didn't shut up...his children. I gagged at the thought of these four black women on the jury allowing themselves to be persuaded into reinforcing my belief that there are no fair trails when we are charged with crimes or when crimes are committed against us.

A part of me has died with this verdict. The bit of hope that allowed me to have the level of tolerance that I once had no longer exists. Nor does the tolerance. I can no longer respectfully and realistically smile in the face of a white police officer without assuming that on February 25, 2000 they were joining in on the festivities. Jumping and clicking their heels as we did for OJ. But the difference, the prints were on the guns, the gloves fit, they were at the scene of the crime, and they admitted to killing a man. And the headlines tomorrow morning will read "Another Nigga Killed by Police. Another Not guilty Verdict. We Did it Again."

As the weeks pass, new instances of the NYPD's civil unrest persist. Week after week New York's minorities are repeatedly raped of their liberties, being murdered by police officers more within one month than in the last year. Innocent lives being taken for granted because of this new found power possessed by the NYPD. Once again I find myself frozen at my desk, staring into nothingness. Wondering when my turn shall come. Or rather, if we shall overcome. Two black men murdered by police officers and one black woman beaten senselessly because she didn't think that the officers who stopped her boyfriend from beating her did

35

an appropriate job of handling the situation. Now we are shot for yelling, shouting, opening the doors of our homes, stepping out of our cars when we are stopped, blinking, smiling, laughing, crying, and buying groceries. We have now become public enemy #1. Wait! We've always been public enemy #1. We no longer feel comfortable in the presence of authorities. When pulled over for speeding we prepare to become victims of more than the typical profiling which the New Jersey State troopers where accused and found guilty of. I can no longer safely practice my freedom of speech and protest. And when talking to a police officer, the words "yes officer" and "yes sir" seem to resemble the words once uttered by our ancestors; "Yes masta'. No masta'." All to avoid being the next person to French kiss a New York City Standard Issue billy club.

Strangely enough, Amadou Diallo got off easy. Abner Loiuma still lives with the memory of his torture. He still has to relive that nightmare. The fact that Diallo may have never known what hit him and why, may have been a blessing in disguise. But here I sit attempting to find some political and social position; searching for the ability to formulate a point of view regarding this painfully spoiled truth about our society. A search that still exists, probably because there is simply no justification for the actions of the NYPD in this situation or any in which they have abused the privileges and authority given to them by their uniforms and badges.

Kicking the Bull

An Unanswered Letter to Black Entertainment Television

I watched powerlessly as she was raped again and again by each one of them. My arms tied behind my back and my chair toppled over on its side. I tried to close my eyes and turn away, but I couldn't. I needed to see the pain that she was experiencing. When they were done, they turned off the lights and walked out. Light pouring in from under the door cast a silhouette on her shivering body. Their voices faded as did their laughter. When nothing remained but silence, I filled it with noise. All I could do was scream for help. My screams went ignored. She lay there in silence.

On Saturday, November 17, 2001, I witnessed something that was truly appalling and disheartening. BET's famous Teen Summit program dedicated an entire show to "Bling." "Bling," representing the "flossiness" and materialism that has emptied the pockets of young African–American men and women while filling the pockets of a mostly white corporate America, was the sole topic of the day's show. The cast members interviewed various artists and executives in and outside of the music industry in order to help define the different aspects of "blinging." They even gave an incorrect definition and description of Hip Hop and the origin of "Bling." Showcasing expensive cars, jewelry, and diamond jewelers throughout the nation was also a focus of the show. In addition, two of the cast members were shown with stylists putting together "Bling" wardrobes for those who don't have budget restrictions and for those who do, although the budget wardrobe still totaled over $600 dollars.

This had to be the poorest taste of programming on BET that I have seen thus far. But proved to be the beginning signs of a sink hole, which took with it a number of mediums and tools that empower Black youth. In light of selling the only Black owned television station to Viacom and firing Tavist Smiley from the network, I am strangely not surprised at the lack of judgment on the part of the network's executives. The state of Black youth is at an all time low. We are struggling within our culture and ourselves. There is a general lack of understanding of the importance of family and Black pride. Our music and music videos have exploited Black women and Black wallets. To dedicate an entire show to "Bling Bling" is unprofessional and unethical. Especially during the state of economic and national emergency that our country is in. Topics such as "African-Americans in the Military," "African-American Communities Affected by the September 11th Attack," "Education about Anthrax and Bio-Terrorism," "Finding Jobs During Economic Slumps," "Introductions to Investing and Financial Security," "REESTABLISHING Family Values," "Respecting Culture and Race," and other issues are more appropriate and needed topics.

I sat and watched the entire program in awe waiting for one of the panelist to begin to discuss how "Bling" has negatively affected our culture and race. I sat waiting for the gears to change, but instead, I received advice on how to properly "Bling" and where to get my "Bling Bling." We are already a race and a culture under much scrutiny. In previous years, BET was the only network that ALLOWED and CELEBRATED black youth that were articulate and spoke intelligently. It is obvious that this celebration is over. All three panelists showed their lack of understanding and knowledge of the English language. I was bombarded with "yanawhaimeans," "hollas," "nowhaimsayins," and "aints." By showing ignorant and clown-like images of us on television, then reinforcing those images with programs that negatively portray the history and culture of those images is continuing to fuel the fire that is already out of control. If this is what selling out to Viacom resulted in, I truly believe that the executives of both companies need to sit down once again and figure out the direction of BET. This type of programming will not be tolerated. If so, I will be among many of BET's former viewers who have chosen to abandon the network and I am positive that I will not be the last. Come on Teen Summit, what happened to "kicking the truth to the young black youth?"

Epilogue: Prelude to Sleeplessness

I only sought closure through this poetry book; closure to chapters of my life that I have long experienced and learned from; chapters that I have grown beyond and grown through. I recall when I was younger; I would sit at the kitchen table with my father, excitedly detailing all of the things I would do when I grew up. He would sit there listening attentively and smiling with pride. When I was done, he'd calmly reply, "You know what they say right? You make plans and God laughs." I would sit there in anger, wondering how this sick fuck could say such a thing to me. My dreams would become deferred before they become heard. It wasn't until years later after experiencing the struggle of college, my first lay off, wondering how tuition was going to be paid while pursuing my MBA, and always seeming to find a way to find a way, that his words finally resonated and actually made sense. God knew my path, but always gave me choices along the way.

So here I am today, wondering what's next and what lies ahead. My words are never planned, but usually reflect the thoughts that I am able to relay while within reach of a pen and paper. I leave voicemails for myself with one-liners who sit around waiting to become two. Weeks later I go back, listening to these bastardized words, shuffled in between messages from my wife, friends, and family members, barely remembering what served as that moment's muse. I've abandoned thousands of ideas that were found and lost within the same instance. Somehow, the few that make it to completion mean something that puts the pieces of this puzzle together. Throughout this book, I've shared with you some of the places I've been; who I was. I only think it fair to shed some light on who I am; who I'm becoming. So this selection, while considered the "Epilogue" or my last words, is more of a beginning; a prelude to sleeplessness or rather a prologue to tomorrow, simply representing the culmination of experiences that equal growth.

Life's End

To my grandfather...I Love You Pops.

Throughout these days, we have laughed

Teary-eyed faces celebrating life it its fullest capacity

But I question and wonder

How can a light that burned so bright suddenly become so dim?

How can a face so round and full become so thin?

How does a smile that once lit up our lives fade with time?

They don't

They remain unchanged in our hearts and minds

The filament of that light infinite and unyielding in its strength

His face still full of life and zest

His smile still implanted in our souls as though it were a brand

We remember Christmases

and birthdays that he'd never forget

11:58PM he would call as if he was the first all day

Stubborn in his ways

Pops, Chuck, Charles, Dad, Granddad, Ferdinand

gave all that he could effortlessly

Only asking that his family remained as close with each other as he did with each of them

Okay, he also wanted his rotisserie

I choose to remember Pops in those joyous moments

The times when he made me laugh

with his Panamanian/Maryland accent

At the breakfast table where he joined in the laughter

while we cracked jokes

laughing at him hysterically

about how he kept us awake with his snores the night before

I remember Pops, full of life and energy

walking to the corner store for empanadas

I remember him as we all should, not in the dimmest light,

but in the brightest and most enjoyable

Emancipation

I have been emancipated by your love

Enduring the joys of this emotional expression

And what we have shared over these years

Is finally being tested

by elements that would hinder another's progression

We are stronger

and we will become greater together

I am on my way

Getting closer everyday

And when I arrive our love will become more glorious

than that for which I have prayed

Our love is unconditional

More spiritual than it is physical

We have walked further together

than most walk individually

You have allowed me to grow freely

while nurturing me with your love

Our souls have been reborn

by thoughts of being one

We have broken shackles

It's beautiful what we have become

We are perfect

Our growth has made this so

Destiny has chosen our paths

and emancipated our souls

We were reborn in this unity

It is beautiful

as our children will be

Created from our love

Created by you and me

Let Freedom Ring

I cut the braids

so I could breathe again

So my hair don't smell like them trees again

I'm free

Long live the revolutionary

This war is lost

because Bush ain't got no support from me

I'm black

1 fourth of this nation of millions

so there is no holding me back

You now need billions

I'm cruising down the Belt Parkway

"Top Down...Chrome spinnin'"

Listening to 1010 WINS

And even they can't tell me if Bin Laden really did it

So I'm to pay for my President's sins

Fukk dat!

I voted for Gore

Only because they wouldn't give Clinton another 4

So now I'm pounding him up in Harlem

Both of us rocking fitted caps over the wavy domes

as the Asian investors buy up all of our old brownstones

My pops got out bided four times this week

by cats that can't even speak

yet alone drive on the right side of this New York City street

I can't be mad at them

because they straight up working in teams

While my black people can't even trust each other enough

to reach these deferred dreams

Raise up Black People

We ain't got nothing if we ain't got each other

You can't trust no one, if you can't trust your brother

Paternal Coma

Today I look at him and realize that I've been mute

A loss of words has come over me

Two years of writer's block

 ultimately reflecting my inability to put this into context

or maybe just a catatonic state

I kiss him on the forehead and cheeks

wondering if he's noticed

I stare at him enamored

Helplessly entranced with thoughts

The day I found out

The first ultrasound

The day he was born

His first independent step

Ironically during the Super Bow

His future and my ability to make it the best it can be for him

He welcomes me with bright eyes and open arms

a beautiful smile

reminding me of the joy and preciousness of life

a thirty inch wingspan

able to comfort my world and all my troubles

a tightened grip

that grabs my fingers and leads me

I follow

But these words are incomplete and helpless

without the tears of my joy to soak the page

Smear the words

Hide my rage

Insignificant banter that I have allowed to brew inside of me

But still nothing will suffice

I watch him grow everyday

assuming that my vocabulary and depth are growing slower

My mind growing older

I have nothing to say

My heart continues stretching

in order to fit a continuously growing love

a little boy that is continuously growing

a bond between father and son that will continue to grow

My child support is to support my child

to be there to support him as he falls throughout life

he will fall throughout life

and I will pick him up when he needs me

I need him

He unknowingly picks me up every day

I wonder if he's noticed the times when he's picked me up

He smiles at me from nowhere

looking at me,

then staring off

as if to say, "I know...I love you too Daddy"

He notices

He knows I struggle for words

so he says nothing

just to make me feel comfortable

I'll talk when he talks

The words will come

...Breathe. Relax. You're awake now. How do you feel?

Acknowledgements

Thank you to the moment's muse and inspirations; for anger, pain, frustration, recklessness, bad decisions, perfect timing, karma, my guardian angel and the Lord who sent him, joy, fear, stress, calm, shrugged shoulders, the beginning, the now, and everything in between or thereafter; for writer's block and the ability to stop long enough to realize what I am going through, why I can't put it on paper, and why I'm not supposed to.

To my friends: Anthony Johnson and V. Quan Lee, incredible writers, thinkers and friends, thank you both for the reviews, advice, and the kind words of inspiration. V. Lee, thanks for that inspiring phone call. Vaughn Johnson (Boogie) for challenging me to be a sick writer when I thought I was already a good one. I respect your grind. Hillary Thomas – my sister/friend, I thought you were different and I found out the truth...I'm grateful and thankful for your ear. Cameron Thompson – brother, friend, business partner; thanks for helping me to find humor in sorrow, pain in joy, rational thoughts in demented situations. Randy, Nigel, Marc, Dale, Trini, Tiffany, Tara, Sahib, Avelyn, Danny, Mike E., Ernst, my Austin people, everyone who's inspired me, read my words, allowed me to jack their emotions or thoughts, and told me that I needed to write a book.

To my family: Tia Lilia and Sean McCants for showing me that it doesn't have to be nuclear to be "clear"; my cousin Alexis who's innocence and glow is contagious; Uncle Ern for being a model of cool and showing me another example of a strong black man and father in the storms of struggle; Nicole and Brendon for holding your dad down; my Grandma Alice who's held family together in the quiet of her wisdom and love; Great Grandma who's wit, humor, and lessons will outlast all of us – and for showing me that perfection can be achieved without 100; Grandma Margie and Aunt Ivy who's collective memory still leaves me in awe; To my extended family the Rampey's – thank you for loving me and allowing me to love you and become family...No words can describe your importance in my life. Dom, I'll tell you what to expect in three months; Justin, only you would go to Thailand and fall in love; Jackie, thank you for always reading the chatter and thank you for the foreword and review. I can't wait until I see you put it down on paper; The Joneses, the Benjamins, the Bells, the Treleavens, the Duttons...Mrs. Harpaul, Mark, and Ingrid, thank you for welcoming me into your lives and family. Thank you Pops. I miss you.

Thank you Nenny Norma for your eyes, ears, and ongoing motivation; my sister Janae for showing me a young woman – strong, beautiful, brave, intelligent, focused, and for helping me to see and appreciate those qualities in the women around me; my father for the review, for giving me the pencils and pads that you boosted from work, and making sure there was never a shortage of lead or ink in the house; my mother, who patiently waited until this was finished. Here it is. I cursed a lot and I know you didn't raise me to speak like this, but wings get dirty when you fly. You said I should fly.

My boys, Joaquin and Tahir, no words can express what you've brought into my life and how its created this man. I'm speechless still, with few clear thoughts about defining fatherhood. One day you will both understand my frustration. I owe you both my life. Tahir, I thank you for sharing your mother with me. Joaquin, I breathe fresh air because you are the rain forest that grows in our home. I Love you both.

Most importantly, I thank my wife Janice, for listening, reading, reviewing, editing, encouraging, understanding, yelling, crying, laughing, smiling, thinking, loving, believing, praying, asking, speaking, accepting, and being my harshest critic, in this book and in life, even when I didn't want to make any changes. Thank you for being my past, my present, and my future inspiration. Thank you for being patient. I Love you more than cooked food.

About the Author

Jamal M. Jones was born in Brooklyn and raised in Queens, New York. It was there that his gift was realized, and with years of heavy influence and support from his parents, family, wife and friends, Jamal's gift of writing was honed and nurtured. During his days he is a Product and Service Marketing Manager, a husband, father, friend, son, brother, and an aspiring poet/writer/entrepreneur. Jamal received his undergraduate degree in Telecommunications (Mass Media) from Morgan State University in Baltimore, Maryland and earned his Master of Business Administration in Marketing Management from St. John's University in Queens, New York Jamal now lives in Austin, Texas with his wife Janice. Together, they have two boys, Joaquin and Tahir. *Mind of a Mad Black Man* is Jamal's first published book of poetry.

Bibliography

[1] "life." *The American Heritage® Dictionary of the English Language, Fourth Edition.* Houghton Mifflin Company, 2004.

[2] "love." Webster's II New Riverside University Dictionary. Houghton Mifflin Company, 1984, 1988.

[3] "love." *The American Heritage® Dictionary of the English Language, Fourth Edition.* Houghton Mifflin Company, 2004.

[4] "the word." Webster's II New Riverside University Dictionary. Houghton Mifflin Company, 1984, 1988.

[5] "the word." Merriam-Webster Online Dictionary. Merriam-Webster, Inc., 2005. http://www.merriam-webster.com .